Contents

KU-754-829

SIMON ARMITAGE

Selected Poems

ff

faber and faber

First published in 2001
by Faber and Faber Limited
Bloomsbury House
74–77 Great Russell Street
London WC1B 3DA

Photoset by Wilmaset Ltd, Birkenhead, Wirral
Printed by Martins the Printers, Berwick-upon-Tweed

A CIP record for this book
is available from the British Library

978–0–571–21076–3

from KILLING TIME (1999)

from THE UNIVERSAL HOME DOCTOR (2002)

from ZOOM!

Snow Joke

Heard the one about the guy from Heaton Mersey?
Wife at home, lover in Hyde, mistress
in Newton-le-Willows and two pretty girls
in the top grade at Werneth prep. Well,

he was late and he had a good car so he snubbed
the police warning-light and tried to finesse
the last six miles of moorland blizzard,
and the story goes he was stuck within minutes.

So he sat there thinking about life and things;
what the dog does when it catches its tail
and about the snake that ate itself to death.
And he watched the windscreen filling up

with snow, and it felt good, and the whisky
from his hip-flask was warm and smooth.
And of course, there isn't a punchline
but the ending goes something like this.

They found him slumped against the steering wheel
with VOLVO printed backwards in his frozen brow.
And they fought in the pub over hot toddies
as to who was to take the most credit.

Him who took the aerial to be a hawthorn twig?
Him who figured out the contour of his car?
Or him who said he heard the horn, moaning
softly like an alarm clock under an eiderdown?

[3]

It Ain't What You Do It's What It Does to You

I have not bummed across America
with only a dollar to spare, one pair
of busted Levi's and a bowie knife.
I have lived with thieves in Manchester.

I have not padded through the Taj Mahal,
barefoot, listening to the space between
each footfall picking up and putting down
its print against the marble floor. But I

skimmed flat stones across Black Moss on a day
so still I could hear each set of ripples
as they crossed. I felt each stones' inertia
spend itself against the water; then sink.

I have not toyed with a parachute chord
while perched on the lip of a light-aircraft;
but I held the wobbly head of a boy
at the day centre, and stroked his fat hands.

And I guess that the tightness in the throat
and the tiny cascading sensation
somewhere inside us are both part of that
sense of something else. That feeling, I mean.

The Bears in Yosemite Park

are busy in the trash cans, grubbing for toothpaste
but the weather on Mam Tor has buckled the road
into Castleton. A crocodile of hikers spills out
into a distant car park as the rain permeates

our innermost teeshirts, and quickly we realise:
this moment is one which will separate some part
of our lives from another. We will always remember
the mobile of seagulls treading water over Edale.

Killer whales pair for life;

they are calling across the base of the ocean
as we sprint for the shelter of the Blue John Mines.
We know the routine. In the most distant cavern
the lights go out and the guide will remind us

that this is true darkness and these splashes
of orange and bristling purple fibre are nothing
but the echoes of light still staining our eyelids.
Back in the car we peel off our sticky layers

and the stacks of rain

are still collapsing sideways as we gear down into
Little Hayfield Please Drive Carefully. On the radio
somebody explains. The bears in Yosemite Park
are swaggering home, legged up with fishing-line

and polythene and above the grind of his skidoo
a ranger curses the politics of skinny-dipping.
This is life. Killer whales are nursing their dead
into quiet waters and we are driving home

in boxer-shorts and bare feet.

And You Know What Thought Did

If you could eat frost, you might think
it would crunch like an apple. You might think

that it forms in fruit like a snowflake forms
in the air. Crisp, and clear. Not so.

Frost in the flesh of an apple runs soft
and brown, and in California they smoke it out

with stove-like affairs that burn wood,
oil, paraffin or coal. Strange then, that

Californian apples are so sweet; so fresh;
because if you could eat smoke you might think

it would taste like a kipper. Not frost.

Poem

Frank O'Hara was open on the desk
but I went straight for the directory.
Nick was out, Joey was engaged, Jim was
just making coffee and why didn't I

come over. I had Astrud Gilberto
singing 'Bim Bom' on my Sony Walkman
and the sun was drying the damp slates on
the rooftops. I walked in without ringing

and he still wasn't dressed or shaved when we
topped up the coffee with his old man's Scotch
(it was only half ten but what the hell)
and took the newspapers into the porch.

Talking Heads were on the radio. I
was just about to mention the football
when he said 'Look, will you help me clear her
wardrobe out?' I said 'Sure Jim, anything.'

A Painted Bird for Thomas Szasz

It was his anorak that first attracted me.
The foam lining was hanging from a split seam
and a tear that ran the length of his back was patched
with sellotape and sticking plaster. So I watched
as he flitted between the front seats of the bus
and fingered the synthetic fur around his hood.

The next time I noticed was at the terminus
where he was pretending to direct the buses.
From then there was a catalogue of incidents,
moments and locations where we coincided,
and each time I watched him talking to the drivers
who ignored him, and jotting down the route numbers.

One particular time he was in the arcade
eyeing the intricacy of a timetable.
He caught me watching the reflection of his face
so he exhaled onto the surface of the glass
and wrote his name on it. Billy. I passed by him,
breathing in, and he smelt like a wet dog, drying.

Another time I noticed more than I meant to
was a lunchtime at the Probation Day Centre
where I squinted through the gap in the serving hatch
to see him watching the traffic on the bypass.
His focus settled on a simple bicycle
which he followed till it slipped below the skyline.

I also saw him, once, in the covered precinct
pissing himself through his pants onto the concrete
and fumbling with the zip on his anorak.
He bothered me, and later I had to walk back
across where the dark circle of his stain had grown
and was still growing, slowly, outward, like a town.

November

We walk to the ward from the badly parked car
with your grandma taking four short steps to our two.
We have brought her here to die and we know it.

You check her towel, soap and family trinkets,
pare her nails, parcel her in the rough blankets
and she sinks down into her incontinence.

It is time John. In their pasty bloodless smiles,
in their slack breasts, their stunned brains and their baldness,
and in us John: we are almost these monsters.

You're shattered. You give me the keys and I drive
through the twilight zone, past the famous station
to your house, to numb ourselves with alcohol.

Inside, we feel the terror of dusk begin.
Outside we watch the evening, failing again,
and we let it happen. We can say nothing.

Sometimes the sun spangles and we feel alive.
One thing we have to get, John, out of this life.

The Civilians

We signed the lease and knew we were landed.
Our dream house: half farm, half mansion; gardens
announcing every approach, a greenhouse
      with a southern aspect.
      Here the sunlight lasted;
evenings stretched their sunburnt arms towards us,
held us in their palms: gilded us, warmed us.

We studied the view as if we owned it;
noted each change, nodded and condoned it.
We rode with the roof down, and if the days
      overstepped themselves
      then the golden evenings
spread like ointment through the open valleys,
buttered one side of our spotless washing.

Forget the dangers of iron pyrites
or the boy who ran from his mother's farm
to the golden house on the other hill
      which was a pigsty
      taking the sunlight.
This was God's glory. The big wheel had stopped
with our chair rocking sweetly at the summit.

For what we have, or had, we are grateful.
      To say otherwise
      would be bitterness
and we know better than to surrender.
Behind the hen-house the jalopy is snookered:
      its bodywork sound,

                its engine buggered
but still there is gold: headlights on the road,
the unchewable crusts of our own loaves,
                old leaves the dog drags in.
                Frost is early this autumn.
                Wrapped up like onions
we shuffle out over the frozen ground;
prop up the line where our sheets are flagging.

The Stuff

We'd heard all the warnings; knew its nicknames.
It arrived in our town by word of mouth
and crackled like wildfire through the grapevine
of gab and gossip. It came from the south

       so we shunned it, naturally;
       sent it to Coventry

and wouldn't have touched it with a barge pole
if it hadn't been at the club one night.
Well, peer group pressure and all that twaddle
so we fussed around it like flies round shite

       and watched,
       and waited

till one kid risked it, stepped up and licked it
and came from every pore in his body.
That clinched it. It snowballed; whirlpooled. Listen,
no one was more surprised than me to be

       cutting it, mixing it,
       snorting and sniffing it

or bulking it up with scouring powder
or chalk, or snuff, or sodium chloride
and selling it under the flyover.
At first we were laughing. It was all right

to be drinking it, eating it,
living and breathing it

but things got seedy; people went missing.
One punter surfaced in the ship-canal
having shed a pair of concrete slippers.
Others were bundled in the back of vans

and were quizzed, thumped,
finished off and dumped

or vanished completely like Weldon Kees:
their cars left idle under the rail bridge
with its cryptic hoarding which stumped the police:
'Oldham – Home of the tubular bandage.'

Others were strangled.
Not that it stopped us.

Someone bubbled us. C.I.D. sussed us
and found some on us. It was cut and dried.
They dusted, booked us, cuffed us and pushed us
down to the station and read us our rights. ·

Possession and supplying:
we had it, we'd had it.

In Court I ambled up and took the oath
and spoke the addict's side of the story.
I said grapevine, barge pole, whirlpool, chloride,
concrete, bandage, station, story. Honest.

Zoom!

It begins as a house, an end terrace
in this case
    but it will not stop there. Soon it is
an avenue
    which cambers arrogantly past the Mechanics' Institute,
turns left
    at the main road without even looking
and quickly it is
    a town with all four major clearing banks,
a daily paper
    and a football team pushing for promotion.

On it goes, oblivious to the Planning Acts,
the green belts,
    and before we know it it is out of our hands:
city, nation,
    hemisphere, universe, hammering out in all directions
until suddenly,
    mercifully, it is drawn aside through the eye
of a black hole
    and bulleted into a neighbouring galaxy, emerging
smaller and smoother
    than a billiard ball but weighing more than Saturn.

People stop me in the street, badger me
in the check-out queue
   and ask 'What is this, this that is so small
and so very smooth
   but whose mass is greater than the ringed planet?'
It's just words
   I assure them. But they will not have it.

from XANADU

§

And you held up the x-ray like an Oscar –
the green light, the all clear, that 'bravo'
from the night porter sending you fox-trotting
into the gift shop: whisky for Victor,

golf balls for Charlie. Some bloody tour: the Seychelles,
India and Quebec, the Hotel Sierra for Pete's sake.
And hadn't you dreamt it – that runaway Alfa Romeo,
the slow crunch, all the sweetness of life dissolving

like sugar in hot tea which you cupped halfheartedly
saying it all in terms of swan songs and curtain calls.
But no, you were A1, OK, no pot needed.
No kilo of plaster to anchor you down

so you framed that negative – the two elegant bones –
the fibula and its friend like dance partners,
the thumbs-up, and your inhaled 'yes'
rushing off through the wards like a rumour,

its echo bouncing back to confirm it.
Clearly, you could see the comeback: London,
November, the Papa Lima Club, no feedback
in the mike, the new troupe in New York Yankee duds,

uniform then peeling to a diamond, a delta
into which you strut, that tango number
with juliet cap and cane, a knockout. Lastly
the exit, and the bitches gather on the balcony

like Zulus as you execute that double cartwheel
into the wings, over and over and out.

§

We thought of Ashfield and imagined trees;
wood smoke, horses and the ricochet of hooves,
a meltwater stream
like milk from the moors,

beehives, bird life, allotments, a breeze.
Like bloodhounds now we track the moment of the truth,
by which I mean
the way we choose

to say which quaver tipped the song into a scream,
to pinpoint how the pinprick widened to a bruise
for you, for me.
I'll list the clues:

the so-called ash, the field, the so-called streets
at sixes, sevens, German shepherds in their schools
of threes
and twos,

for peace of mind this baseball bat, for sleep
these tablets and a certain ratio of booze
will count for sheep
and see us through.

We idle now on waiting lists, and dream
of runways, level crossings, traffic queues;
waiting to come clean,
to break the news

of how we live, of what we have seen,
of how it leaves us, and what that proves.
A light goes green,
but nobody moves.

from KID

Gooseberry Season

Which reminds me. He appeared
at noon, asking for water. He'd walked from town
after losing his job, leaving a note for his wife and his brother
and locking his dog in the coal bunker.
We made him a bed

and he slept till Monday.
A week went by and he hung up his coat.
Then a month, and not a stroke of work, a word of thanks,
a farthing of rent or a sign of him leaving.
One evening he mentioned a recipe

for smooth, seedless gooseberry sorbet
but by then I was tired of him: taking pocket money
from my boy at cards, sucking up to my wife and on his last night
sizing up my daughter. He was smoking my pipe
as we stirred his supper.

Where does the hand become the wrist?
Where does the neck become the shoulder? The watershed
and then the weight, whatever turns up and tips us over that
    razor's edge
between something and nothing, between
one and the other.

I could have told him this
but didn't bother. We ran him a bath
and held him under, dried him off and dressed him
and loaded him into the back of the pick-up.
Then we drove without headlights

to the county boundary,
dropped the tailgate, and after my boy
had been through his pockets we dragged him like a mattress
across the meadow and on the count of four
threw him over the border.

This is not general knowledge, except
in gooseberry season, which reminds me, and at the table
I have been known to raise an eyebrow, or scoop the sorbet
into five equal portions, for the hell of it.
I mention this for a good reason.

True North

Hitching home for the first time, the last leg
being a bummed ride in a cold guard's van
through the unmanned stations to a platform
iced with snow. It's not much to crow about,

the trip from one term at Portsmouth Poly,
all that Falklands business still to come. From there
the village looked stopped; a clutch of houses
in a toy snow-storm with the dust settled

and me ready to stir it, loaded up
with a haul of new facts, half expecting
flags or bunting, a ticker-tape welcome,
a fanfare or a civic reception.

In the Old New Inn two men sat locked
in an arm-wrestle – their one combined fist
dithered like a compass needle. Later,
after Easter, they would ask me outside

for saying Malvinas in the wrong place
at the wrong time, but that night was Christmas
and the drinks were on them. Christmas! At home
I hosted a new game: stretch a tissue

like a snare drum over a brandy glass,
put a penny on, spark up, then take turns
to dimp burning cigs through the diaphragm
before the tissue gives, the penny drops.

As the guests yawned their heads off I lectured
about wolves: how they mass on the shoreline
of Bothnia, wait for the weather, then
make the crossing when the Gulf heals over.

Brassneck

United, mainly,
every odd Saturday,
or White Hart Lane for a worthwhile away game.
Down in the crowds at the grounds where the bread is:
the gold, the plastic,
the cheque-books, the readies,

the biggest fish
or the easiest meat,
or both. Consider that chap we took last week:
we turned him over and walked off the terrace
with a grand exactly
in dog-eared tenners;

takings like that
don't get reported.
Carter, he's a sort of junior partner;
it's two seasons now since we first teamed up
in the Stretford End
in the FA Cup;

it was all United
when I caught him filching
my cigarette case, and he felt me fishing
a prial of credit cards out of his britches.
Since that day
we've worked these pitches.

We tend to kick off
by the hot dog vans

[31]

and we've lightened a good many fair-weather fans
who haven't a clue where to queue for tickets.
Anything goes, if it's
loose we lift it.

At City last year
in the derby match
we did the right thing with a smart-looking lass
who'd come unhitched in the crush from her friend.
We escorted her out
of the Platt Lane End,

arm in arm
along the touchline,
past the tunnel and out through the turnstile
and directed her on to a distant police car.
I did the talking
and Carter fleeced her.

As Carter once put it:
when we're on the ball
we can clean someone out, from a comb to a coil,
and we need nine eyes to watch for the coppers
though at Goodison Park
when I got collared

two bright young bobbies
took me into the toilets
and we split the difference. Bent policemen;
there's always a couple around when you need them.
It's usually Autumn
when we loosen our fingers

at the Charity Shield
which is pretty big business
though semis and finals are birthdays and Christmas.
Hillsborough was a different ball game of course;
we'd started early,
then saw what the score was,

so we turned things in
as a mark of respect,
just kept enough back to meet certain expenses
(I'm referring here to a red and blue wreath;
there are trading standards,
even for thieves).

Carter keeps saying
he'd be quick to wager
that worse things go on in the name of wages,
but I've let Carter know there's a place and a time
to say as we speak,
speak as we find.

Speaking of Carter,
and not that I mind,
he thinks I'm a touch on the gingery side:
my voice a little too tongued and grooved,
my locks a little
too washed and groomed,

my cuticles tenderly
pushed back and pruned,
both thumbnails capped with a full half-moon,
each fingernail manicured, pared and polished...
We can work hand in hand if we stick to the rules:

[33]

he keeps his cunt-hooks out of my wallet,
I keep my tentacles
out of his pocket.

You May Turn Over and Begin . . .

'Which of these films was Dirk Bogarde
not in? One hundredweight of bauxite

makes how much aluminium?
How many tales in *The Decameron?*'

General Studies, the upper sixth, a doddle, a cinch
for anyone with an ounce of common sense

or a calculator
with a memory feature.

Having galloped through but not caring enough
to check or double-check, I was dreaming of

milk-white breasts and nakedness, or more specifically
virginity.

That term – everybody felt the heat
but the girls were having none of it:

long and cool like cocktails,
out of reach, their buns and pigtails

only let out for older guys with studded jackets
and motor-bikes and spare helmets.

One jot of consolation
was the tall spindly girl riding pillion

on her man's new Honda
who, with the lights at amber,

put down both feet and stood to stretch her limbs,
to lift the visor and push back her fringe

and to smooth her tight jeans.
As he pulled off down the street

she stood there like a wishbone,
high and dry, her legs wide open,

and rumour has it he didn't notice
till he came round in the ambulance

having underbalanced on a tight left-hander.
A Taste of Honey. Now I remember.

At Sea

It is not through weeping,
but all evening the pale blue eye
on your most photogenic side has kept
its own unfathomable tide. Like the boy
at the dyke I have been there:

held out a huge finger,
lifted atoms of dust with the point
of a tissue and imagined slivers of hair
in the oil on the cornea. We are both
in the dark, but I go on

drawing the eyelid up by its lashes,
folding it almost inside-out, then finding
and hiding every mirror in the house
as the iris, besieged with the ink
of blood rolls back

into its own orbit. Nothing
will help it. Through until dawn
you dream the true story of the boy
who hooked out his eye and ate it,
so by six in the morning

I am steadying the ointment
that will bite like an onion, piping
a line of cream while avoiding the pupil
and in no time it is glued shut
like a bad mussel.

Friends call round
and mean well. They wait
and whisper in the air-lock of the lobby
with patches, eyewash, the truth
about mascara.

Even the cats are on to it;
they bring in starlings, and because their feathers
are the colours of oil on water in sunlight
they are a sign of something.
In the long hours

beyond us, irritations heal
into arguments. For the eighteenth time
it comes to this: the length of your leg sliding out
from the covers, the ball of your foot
like a fist on the carpet

while downstairs
I cannot bring myself to hear it.
Words have been spoken; things that were bottled
have burst open and to walk in now
would be to walk in

on the ocean.

Poem

And if it snowed and snow covered the drive
he took a spade and tossed it to one side.
And always tucked his daughter up at night.
And slippered her the one time that she lied.

And every week he tipped up half his wage.
And what he didn't spend each week he saved.
And praised his wife for every meal she made.
And once, for laughing, punched her in the face.

And for his mum he hired a private nurse.
And every Sunday taxied her to church.
And he blubbed when she went from bad to worse.
And twice he lifted ten quid from her purse.

Here's how they rated him when they looked back:
sometimes he did this, sometimes he did that.

Kid

Batman, big shot, when you gave the order
to grow up, then let me loose to wander
leeward, freely through the wild blue yonder
as you liked to say, or ditched me, rather,
in the gutter ... well, I turned the corner.
Now I've scotched that 'he was like a father
to me' rumour, sacked it, blown the cover
on that 'he was like an elder brother'
story, let the cat out on that caper
with the married woman, how you took her
downtown on expenses in the motor.
Holy robin-redbreast-nest-egg-shocker!
Holy roll-me-over-in-the-clover,
I'm not playing ball boy any longer
Batman, now I've doffed that off-the-shoulder
Sherwood-Forest-green and scarlet number
for a pair of jeans and crew-neck jumper;
now I'm taller, harder, stronger, older.
Batman, it makes a marvellous picture:
you without a shadow, stewing over
chicken giblets in the pressure cooker,
next to nothing in the walk-in larder,
punching the palm of your hand all winter,
you baby, now I'm the real boy wonder.

Abstracting Electricity

So that's that, global warming and the ozone hole
and how the season scorched the town's main reservoir
slowly down its backbone of benchmarks. Atlantis, we reckon,
as we wander through the crater and scratch around
half-heartedly for keepsakes, or hopscotch over the topsoil

which is broken and baked into perfect octagonal cakes.
There's an echo; let's talk for the sake of it. Language,
we know, is less use than half a scissor, so ramble on
past the bridge and the pumping-station where that life-buoy
hoopla-ed over the rain-gauge is a statement, and the shadows

of hang-gliders down in the valley are pterodactyls.
Or impress me with your first date, how he took you
to the rink but couldn't skate so you linked him
clockwise at a gentle pace. Later, unravelling
that sacred fiver from your grandmother's locket,

you stood the price of a pineapple sundae, two spoons,
and thawed out in the photo booth and split the prints –
your eyes gone red in the flash like the devil's.
Or blame it on a blip in your biorhythms:
how you're dead on your feet all day but at night

you can't unplug. A course of tablets does the trick
but your hair falls out in lumps so you dump it.
You take a job but it doesn't suit so you sack it.
You buy that car, a wreck with three months' tax and test
and tyres so bald that you drive on a penny and know

if it's heads or tails, the bonnet maloccluded from that brush
with the business end of a JCB, we lift both feet
when you run through a puddle; that bad. And the house:
remind me how you lapped copper wire round the meter,
    halved
the bills, hung shirts in the fridge from May to September.

And the platitudes: one standpipe doesn't make a summer,
the lead in a gallon of petrol wouldn't fill the teat
of a baby's bottle, which is small, though you wouldn't want it
as a wart at the end of your nose, sprung up overnight,
unsightly whichever side you see it from, unspeakable

but there on the tip of your tongue.

Great Sporting Moments: The Treble

The rich! I love them. Trust them to suppose
the gift of tennis is deep in their bones.

Those chaps from the coast with all their own gear
from electric eyes to the umpire's chair,

like him whose arse I whipped with five choice strokes
perfected on West Yorkshire's threadbare courts:

a big first serve that strained his alloy frame,
a straight return that went back like a train,

a lob that left him gawping like a fish,
a backhand pass that kicked and drew a wisp

of chalk, a smash like a rubber bullet
and a bruise to go with it. Three straight sets.

Smarting in the locker rooms he offered
double or quits; he was a born golfer

and round the links he'd wipe the floor with me.
I played the ignoramus to a tee:

the pleb in the gag who asked the viscount
what those eggcup-like things were all about –

'They're to rest my balls on when I'm driving.'
'Blimey, guv, Rolls-Royce think of everything' –

but at the fifth when I hadn't faltered
he lost his rag and threw down the gauntlet;

we'd settle this like men: with the gloves on.
I said, no, no, no, no, no, no, no. OK, come on then.

Lines Thought to Have Been Written
on the Eve of the Execution of a Warrant
for His Arrest

Boys, I have a feeling in my water,
in my bones, that should we lose our houses
and our homes, our jobs, or just in general
come unstuck, she will not lend one button
from her blouse, and from her kitchen garden
not one bean. But through farmyards and dust bowls
we will lay down our topcoats, or steel ourselves
and bare our backs over streams and manholes.

Down Birdcage Walk in riots or wartime
we will not hear of her hitching her skirt
or see for ourselves that frantic footwork,
busy like a swan's beneath the surface.
But quickly our tank will stop in its tracks;
they'll turn the turret lid back like a stone;
inside, our faces set like flint, her name
cross-threaded in the barrels of our throats.

I have this from reliable sources:
boys, with our letters, our first class honours
and diplomas we are tenfold brighter
than her sons and daughters put together.
But someone hangs on every word they speak,
and let me mention here the hummingbird
that seems suspended at the orchid's lips,
or else the bird that picks the hippo's teeth.

Boys, if we burn, she will not pass one drop
of water over us, and if we drown
she will not let a belt or bootlace down,
or lend a hand. She'll turn instead and show
a leg, a stocking, sheer and ladderless.
And even then we will not lose our heads
by mouthing an air bubble out of turn
or spouting a smoke ring against her name.

But worse than this, in handouts and speeches
she will care for us, and cannot mean it.
Picture the stroke of the hour that takes her:
our faces will freeze as if the wind had changed,
we shall hear in our hearts a note, a murmur,
and talk in terms of where we stood, how struck,
how still we were the moment this happened,
in good faith, as if it really mattered.

Not the Furniture Game

His hair was a crow fished out of a blocked chimney
and his eyes were boiled eggs with the tops hammered in
and his blink was a cat flap
and his teeth were bluestones or Easter Island statues
and his bite was a perfect horseshoe.
His nostrils were both barrels of a shotgun, loaded.
And his mouth was an oil exploration project gone bankrupt
and his last smile was a caesarean section
and his tongue was an iguanodon
and his whistle was a laser beam
and his laugh was a bad case of kennel cough.
He coughed, and it was malt whisky.
And his headaches were Arson in Her Majesty's Dockyards
and his arguments were outboard motors strangled with fishing-line
and his neck was a bandstand
and his Adam's apple was a ball cock
and his arms were milk running off from a broken bottle.
His elbows were boomerangs or pinking shears.
And his wrists were ankles
and his handshakes were puff adders in the bran tub
and his fingers were astronauts found dead in their spacesuits
and the palms of his hands were action paintings
and both thumbs were blue touchpaper.
And his shadow was an opencast mine.
And his dog was a sentry-box with no one in it
and his heart was a first world war grenade discovered by children
and his nipples were timers for incendiary devices
and his shoulder-blades were two butchers at the
    meat-cleaving competition
and his belly-button was the Falkland Islands

and his private parts were the Bermuda triangle
and his backside was a priest hole
and his stretchmarks were the tide going out.
The whole system of his blood was Dutch elm disease.
And his legs were depth charges
and his knees were fossils waiting to be tapped open
and his ligaments were rifles wrapped in oilcloth under the
    floorboards
and his calves were the undercarriages of Shackletons.
The balls of his feet were where meteorites had landed
and his toes were a nest of mice under the lawn-mower.
And his footprints were Vietnam
and his promises were hot-air balloons floating off over the
    trees
and his one-liners were footballs through other people's
    windows
and his grin was the Great Wall of China as seen from the
    moon
and the last time they talked, it was apartheid.

She was a chair, tipped over backwards
with his donkey jacket on her shoulders.

They told him,
and his face was a hole
where the ice had not been thick enough to hold her.

Robinson's Resignation

Because I am done with this thing called work,
the paper-clips and staples of it all.
The customers and their huge excuses,
their incredulous lies and their beautiful
foul-mouthed daughters. I am swimming with it,
right up to here with it. And I am bored,
bored like the man who married a mermaid.

And I am through with the business of work.
In meetings, with the minutes, I have dreamed
and doodled, drifted away then undressed
and dressed almost every single woman,
every button, every zip and buckle.
For eighteen months in this diving-helmet
I have lived with the stench of my own breath.

So I am finished with the whole affair.
As for this friendship thing, I couldn't give
a weeping fig for those so-called brothers
who are all voltage, no current. I have
emptied my locker. I should like to leave
and to fold things now like a pair of gloves
or two clean socks, one into the other.

This is my final word. Nothing will follow.

About His Person

Five pounds fifty in change, exactly,
a library card on its date of expiry.

A postcard, stamped,
unwritten, but franked,

a pocket-size diary slashed with a pencil
from March twenty-fourth to the first of April.

A brace of keys for a mortise lock,
an analogue watch, self-winding, stopped.

A final demand
in his own hand,

a rolled-up note of explanation
planted there like a spray carnation

but beheaded, in his fist.
A shopping list.

A giveaway photograph stashed in his wallet,
a keepsake banked in the heart of a locket.

No gold or silver,
but crowning one finger

a ring of white unweathered skin.
That was everything.

from BOOK OF MATCHES

from Book of Matches

My party piece:
I strike, then from the moment when the matchstick
conjures up its light, to when the brightness moves
beyond its means, and dies, I say the story
of my life –

dates and places, torches I carried,
a cast of names and faces, those
who showed me love, or came close,
the changes I made, the lessons I learnt –

then somehow still find time to stall and blush
before I'm bitten by the flame, and burnt.

A warning, though, to anyone nursing
an ounce of sadness, anyone alone:
don't try this on your own; it's dangerous,
madness.

★

Mother, any distance greater than a single span
requires a second pair of hands.
You come to help me measure windows, pelmets, doors,
the acres of the walls, the prairies of the floors.

You at the zero-end, me with the spool of tape, recording
length, reporting metres, centimetres back to base, then
   leaving
up the stairs, the line still feeding out, unreeling
years between us. Anchor. Kite.

I space-walk through the empty bedrooms, climb
the ladder to the loft, to breaking point, where something
has to give;
two floors below your fingertips still pinch
the last one-hundredth of an inch ... I reach
towards a hatch that opens on an endless sky
to fall or fly.

★

My father thought it bloody queer,
the day I rolled home with a ring of silver in my ear
half hidden by a mop of hair. 'You've lost your head.
If that's how easily you're led
you should've had it through your nose instead.'

And even then I hadn't had the nerve to numb
the lobe with ice, then drive a needle through the skin,
then wear a safety-pin. It took a jeweller's gun
to pierce the flesh, and then a friend
to thread a sleeper in, and where it slept
the hole became a sore, became a wound, and wept.

At twenty-nine, it comes as no surprise to hear
my own voice breaking like a tear, released like water,
cried from way back in the spiral of the ear. *If I were you,*
I'd take it out and leave it out next year.

★

I am very bothered when I think
of the bad things I have done in my life.
Not least that time in the chemistry lab
when I held a pair of scissors by the blades
and played the handles
in the naked lilac flame of the Bunsen burner;
then called your name, and handed them over.

O the unrivalled stench of branded skin
as you slipped your thumb and middle finger in,
then couldn't shake off the two burning rings. Marked,
the doctor said, for eternity.

Don't believe me, please, if I say
that was just my butterfingered way, at thirteen,
of asking you if you would marry me.

★

Brung up with swine, I was,
and dogs,
and raised on a diet of slime and slops
and pobs, then fell in one day
with a different kind. Some say

that gives me the right
to try out that line
about having a bark and having a bite,
and a nose for uncovering truffles, or shite.
Or, put another way,

what looks from afar
like a cloak of fur
is a coat of hair. Cut back the hair to find
not skin, but rind.

★

Those bastards in their mansions:
to hear them shriek, you'd think
I'd poisoned the dogs and vaulted the ditches,
crossed the lawns in stocking feet and threadbare britches,
forced the door of one of the porches, and lifted
the gift of fire from the burning torches,

then given heat and light to streets and houses,
told the people how to ditch their cuffs and shackles,
armed them with the iron from their wrists and ankles.

Those lords and ladies in their palaces and castles,
they'd have me sniffed out by their beagles,
picked at by their eagles, pinned down, grilled
beneath the sun.

Me, I stick to the shadows, carry a gun.

★

æŋkɪˈləʊzɪŋ spɒndɪˈlaɪtɪs:
ankylosing meaning bond or join,
and spondylitis meaning of the bone or spine.
That half explains the cracks and clicks,
the clockwork of my joints and discs,
the ratchet of my hips. I'm fossilizing –
every time I rest
I let the gristle knit, weave, mesh.

My dear, my skeleton will set like biscuit overnight,
like glass, like ice, and you can choose
to snap me back to life before first light,
or let me laze until
the shape I take becomes the shape I keep.

Don't leave me be. Don't let me sleep.

★

I've made out a will; I'm leaving myself
to the National Health. I'm sure they can use
the jellies and tubes and syrups and glues,
the web of nerves and veins, the loaf of brains,
an assortment of fillings and stitches and wounds,
blood – a gallon exactly of bilberry soup –
the chassis or cage or cathedral of bone;
but not the heart, they can leave that alone.

They can have the lot, the whole stock:
the loops and coils and sprockets and springs and rods,
the twines and cords and strands,
the face, the case, the cogs and the hands,

but not the pendulum, the ticker;
leave that where it stops or hangs.

★

No convictions – that's my one major fault.
Nothing to tempt me to scream and shout, nothing
to raise Cain or make a song and dance about.

A man like me could be a real handful,
steeping himself overnight in petrol,
becoming inflamed on behalf of the world,
letting his blood boil, letting his hair curl.

I have a beauty spot three inches south-east
of my nose, a heart that has to be a match
for any pocket watch, a fist
that opens like a fine Swiss Army knife,
and certain tricks that have been known
to bring about spontaneous applause.
But no cause, no cause.

★

Some unimportant word or phrase
runs through my mind, on and off, for days.
Light the blue touch and stand well back.
Never return to a smouldering jumping jack.

Tonight I'm blank, burnt out, parked
in the garage, with the engine running, in the dark.
The ones who know me hold me at arm's length,
the others want to see me dead.

Not yet.
I tear the last match from the book,
fetch it hard and once
across the windscreen. In the glass

I'm taken with myself, caught in the act –
conducting light, until the heat licks
up against my thumb and fingertips, unlocks
my hand, gives me a start, trips

something in the flashbulb of my heart.

Map Reference

Not that it was the first peak in the range,
or the furthest.
It didn't have the swankiest name
and wasn't the highest even, or the finest.

In fact, if those in the know
ever had their say about sea-level or cross-sections,
or had their way with angles and vectors,
or went there with their instruments about them,
it might have been more of a hill than a mountain.

As for its features,
walls fell into stones along its lower reaches,
fields ran up against its footslopes, scree had loosened
from around its shoulders. Incidentally, pine trees
pitched about its south and west approaches.

We could have guessed, I think, had we taken to it,
the view, straightforward, from its summit.

So,
as we rounded on it from the road that day,
how very smart of me to say or not to say
what we both knew:
that it stood where it stood, so absolutely, for you.

To Poverty
(after Laycock)

You are near again, and have been there
or thereabouts for years. Pull up a chair.
I'd know that shadow anywhere, that silhouette
without a face, that shape. Well, be my guest.
We'll live like sidekicks – hip to hip,
like Siamese twins, joined at the pocket.

I've tried too long to see the back of you.
Last winter when you came down with the flu
I should have split, cut loose, but
let you pass the buck, the bug. Bad blood.
It's cold again; come closer to the fire, the light,
and let me make you out.

How have you hurt me, let me count the ways:
the months of Sundays
when you left me in the damp, the dark,
the red, or down and out, or out of work.
The weeks on end of bread without butter,
bed without supper.

That time I fell through Schofield's shed
and broke both legs,
and Schofield couldn't spare to split
one stick of furniture to make a splint.
Thirteen weeks I sat there till they set.
What can the poor do but wait? And wait.

How come you're struck with me? Go see the Queen,
lean on the doctor or the dean,
breathe on the major,
squeeze the mason or the manager,
go down to London, find a novelist at least
to bother with, to bleed, to leech.

On second thoughts, stay put.
A person needs to get a person close enough
to stab him in the back.
Robert Frost said that. Besides,
I'd rather keep you in the corner of my eye
than wait for you to join me side by side
at every turn, on every street, in every town.
Sit down. I said sit down.

Parable of the Dead Donkey

Instructions arrived by registered post
under cover of separate envelopes:
directions first
to pinpoint the place
in the shape of maps and compass bearings;
those, then forms and stamps for loss of earnings.
So much was paid
to diggers of graves
by keepers or next of kin, per leg
(which made for the dumping of quadrupeds):
sixteen quid
to send off a pig
or sink a pit for a dog or pony.
But less to plant a man than a donkey.
Cheaper by half
for a pregnant horse
that died with all four hooves inside her
than one with a stillborn foal beside her.
And this was a bind,
being duty bound
where ownership was unestablished.
We filled the flasks and loaded the Transit,
then set out, making
for the undertaking.

Facing north, he was dead at three o'clock
in a ring of meadow grass, closely cropped,
where a metal chain
on a wooden stake
had stopped him ambling off at an angle,

worn him down in a perfect circle.
We burrowed in
right next to him
through firm white soil. An hour's hard labour
took us five feet down – and then the weather:
thunder biting
the heels of lightning,
a cloudburst drawing a curtain of rain
across us, filling the bath of the grave,
and we waded in it
for one more minute,
dredged and shovelled as the tide was rising,
bailed out for fear of drowning, capsizing.
Back on top
we weighed him up,
gave some thought to this beast of the Bible:
the nose and muzzle, the teeth, the eyeballs,
the rump, the hindquarters,
the flanks, the shoulders,
everything soothed in the oil of the rain –
the eel of his tongue, the keel of his spine,
the rope of his tail,
the weeds of his mane.
Then we turned him about and slipped his anchor,
eased him out of the noose of his tether,
and rolled him in
and started to dig.
But even with donkey, water and soil
there wasn't enough to level the hole
after what was washed away
or turned into clay
or trodden in, so we opened the earth
and started in on a second trench for dirt

to fill the first.
Which left a taste
of starting something that wouldn't finish:
a covered grave with a donkey in it,
a donkey-size hole
within a stone's throw
and not a single bone to drop in it
or a handful of dust to toss on top of it.

The van wouldn't start, so we wandered home
on foot, in the dark, without supper or profit.

Hitcher

I'd been tired, under
the weather, but the ansaphone kept screaming:
One more sick-note, mister, and you're finished. Fired.
I thumbed a lift to where the car was parked.
A Vauxhall Astra. It was hired.

I picked him up in Leeds.
He was following the sun to west from east
with just a toothbrush and the good earth for a bed. The truth,
he said, was blowin' in the wind,
or round the next bend.

I let him have it
on the top road out of Harrogate – once
with the head, then six times with the krooklok
in the face – and didn't even swerve.
I dropped it into third

and leant across
to let him out, and saw him in the mirror
bouncing off the kerb, then disappearing down the verge.
We were the same age, give or take a week.
He'd said he liked the breeze

to run its fingers
through his hair. It was twelve noon.
The outlook for the day was moderate to fair.
Stitch that, I remember thinking,
you can walk from there.

To His Lost Lover

Now they are no longer
any trouble to each other

he can turn things over, get down to that list
of things that never happened, all of the lost

unfinishable business.
For instance ... for instance,

how he never clipped and kept her hair, or drew a hairbrush
through that style of hers, and never knew how not to blush

at the fall of her name in close company.
How they never slept like buried cutlery –

two spoons or forks cupped perfectly together,
or made the most of some heavy weather –

walked out into hard rain under sheet lightning,
or did the gears while the other was driving.

How he never raised his fingertips
to stop the segments of her lips

from breaking the news,
or tasted the fruit,

or picked for himself the pear of her heart,
or lifted her hand to where his own heart

was a small, dark, terrified bird
in her grip. Where it hurt.

Or said the right thing,
or put it in writing.

And never fled the black mile back to his house
before midnight, or coaxed another button of her blouse,

then another,
or knew her

favourite colour,
her taste, her flavour,

and never ran a bath or held a towel for her,
or soft-soaped her, or whipped her hair

into an ice-cream cornet or a beehive
of lather, or acted out of turn, or misbehaved

when he might have, or worked a comb
where no comb had been, or walked back home

through a black mile hugging a punctured heart,
where it hurt, where it hurt, or helped her hand

to his butterfly heart
in its two blue halves.

And never almost cried,
and never once described

an attack of the heart,
or under a silk shirt

nursed in his hand her breast,
her left, like a tear of flesh

wept by the heart,
where it hurts,

or brushed with his thumb the nut of her nipple,
or drank intoxicating liquors from her navel.

Or christened the Pole Star in her name,
or shielded the mask of her face like a flame,

a pilot light,
or stayed the night,

or steered her back to that house of his,
or said 'Don't ask me to say how it is

I like you.
I just might do.'

How he never figured out a fireproof plan,
or unravelled her hand, as if her hand

were a solid ball
of silver foil

and discovered a lifeline hiding inside it,
and measured the trace of his own alongside it.

But said some things and never meant them –
sweet nothings anybody could have mentioned.

And left unsaid some things he should have spoken,
about the heart, where it hurt exactly, and how often.

Becoming of Age

The year the institutions would not hold.
The autumn when the convicts took their leave.
The month the radio went haywire, gargled
through the long-range forecast, and their names.
The fortnight of the curfew, and the cheese-wire
of the Klaxon slicing day from night, night
from day. The clear, unclouded ocean

of the sky. The week we met. The afternoon
we might have seen a ghost, a scarecrow
striding boldly down The Great North Road
towards us, wearing everything he owned.

The minute in the phone box with the coin,
the dialling tone, the disagreement – heads
to turn him in to the authorities, or tails
to leave him be, to let him go to ground
and keep the public footpaths trodden down,
the green lanes and the bridleways.

Then on the glass, each in its own time – one,
two, three, four, five, six fingerprints of rain.

from THE DEAD SEA POEMS

The Dead Sea Poems

And I was travelling lightly, barefoot
over bedrock, then through lands that were stitched
with breadplant and camomile. Or was it

burdock. For a living I was driving
a river of goats towards clean water,
when one of the herd cut loose to a cave

on the skyline. To flush it out, I shaped
a sling from a length of cotton bandage,
or was it a blanket, then launched a rock

at the target, which let out a racket –
the tell-tale sound of man-made objects.
Inside the cave like a set of skittles

stood a dozen caskets, and each one gasped –
a little theatrically perhaps –
when opened, then gave out a breath of musk

and pollen, and reaching down through cool sand
I found poems written in my own hand.
Being greatly in need of food and clothing,

and out of pocket, I let the lot go
for twelve times nothing, but saw them again
this spring, on public display, out of reach

under infra-red and ultra-sonic,
apparently worth an absolute packet.
Knowing now the price of my early art

I have gone some way towards taking it all
to heart, by bearing it all in mind, like
praying, saying it over and over

at night, by singing the whole of the work
to myself, every page of that innocent,
everyday, effortless verse, of which this

is the first.

Man with a Golf Ball Heart

They set about him with a knife and fork, I heard,
and spooned it out. Dunlop, dimpled, perfectly hard.
It bounced on stone but not on softer ground – they made
a note of that. They slit the skin – a leathery,
rubbery, eyelid thing – and further in, three miles
of gut or string, elastic. Inside that, a pouch
or sac of pearl-white balm or gloss, like Copydex.
It weighed in at the low end of the litmus test
but wouldn't burn, and tasted bitter, bad, resin
perhaps from a tree or plant. And it gave off gas
that caused them all to weep when they inspected it.

That heart had been an apple once, they reckoned. Green.
They had a scheme to plant an apple there again
beginning with a pip, but he rejected it.

I Say I Say I Say

Anyone here had a go at themselves
for a laugh? Anyone opened their wrists
with a blade in the bath? Those in the dark
at the back, listen hard. Those at the front
in the know, those of us who have, hands up,
let's show that inch of lacerated skin
between the forearm and the fist. Let's tell it
like it is: strong drink, a crimson tidemark
round the tub, a yard of lint, white towels
washed a dozen times, still pink. Tough luck.
A passion then for watches, bangles, cuffs.
A likely story: you were lashed by brambles
picking berries from the woods. Come clean, come good,
repeat with me the punch line 'Just like blood'
when those at the back rush forward to say
how a little love goes a long long long way.

White Christmas

For once it is a white Christmas,
so white the roads are impassable
and my wife is snowbound
in a town untroubled by tractor or snowplough.
In bed, awake, alone. She calls

and we pass on our presents by telephone.
Mine is a watch, the very one
I would have chosen. Hers is a song,
the one with the line *Here come the hills of time*
and it sits in its sleeve,

unsung and unopened. But the dog downstairs
is worrying, gnawing, howling,
so I walk her through clean snow
along the tow-path to the boat-house at a steady pace,
then to my parents' place

where my mother is Marie Curie, in the kitchen
discovering radium, and my father is Fred Flintstone,
and a guest from the past has a look on her face meaning
lie and I'll have your teeth for a necklace, boy,
your eyeballs for earrings,

your bullshit for breakfast,
and my two-year-old niece is baby Jesus,
passing between us with the fruit of the earth
and the light of the world – Christingle – a blood orange
spiked with a burning candle.

We eat, but the dog begs at the table,
drinks from the toilet, sings in the cellar.
Only baby Jesus wanders with me down the stairs
with a shank of meat to see her, to feed her.
Later, when I stand to leave

my father wants to shake me by the hand
but my arms are heavy, made of a base metal,
and the dog wants to take me down the black lane, back
to an empty house again. A car goes by
with my sister inside

and to wave goodnight
she lifts the arm of the sleeping infant Christ,
but I turn my wrist to notice the time. There and then
I'm the man in the joke, the man in a world of friends
where all the clocks are stopped,

synchronising his own watch.

Before You Cut Loose,

                         put dogs on the list
of difficult things to lose. Those dogs ditched
on the North York Moors or the Sussex Downs
or hurled like bags of sand from rented cars
have followed their noses to market towns
and bounced like balls into their owners' arms.
I heard one story of a dog that swam
to the English coast from the Isle of Man,
and a dog that carried eggs and bacon
and a morning paper from the village
surfaced umpteen leagues and two years later,
bacon eaten but the eggs unbroken,
newsprint dry as tinder, to the letter.
A dog might wander the width of the map
to bury its head in its owner's lap,
crawl the last mile to dab a bleeding paw
against its own front door. To die at home,
a dog might walk its four legs to the bone.
You can take off the tag and the collar
but a dog wears one coat and one colour.
A dog got rid of – that's a dog for life.
No dog howls like a dog kicked out at night.
Try looking a dog like that in the eye.

Goalkeeper with a Cigarette

That's him in the green, green cotton jersey,
prince of the clean sheets – some upright insect
boxed between the sticks, the horizontal
and the pitch, stood with something up his sleeve,
armed with a pouch of tobacco and skins
to roll his own, or else a silver tin
containing eight or nine already rolled.
That's him with one behind his ear, between
his lips, or one tucked out of sight and lit –
a stamen cupped in the bud of his fist.
That's him sat down, not like those other clowns,
performing acrobatics on the bar, or press-ups
in the box, or running on the spot,
togged out in turtleneck pyjama-suits
with hands as stunted as a bunch of thumbs,
hands that are bandaged or swaddled with gloves,
laughable, frying-pan, sausage-man gloves.
Not my man, though, that's not what my man does;
a man who stubs his reefers on the post
and kicks his heels in the stud-marks and butts,
lighting the next from the last, in one breath
making the save of the year with his legs,
taking back a deep drag on the goal-line
in the next; on the one hand throwing out
or snaffling the ball from a high corner,
flicking off loose ash with the other. Or
in the freezing cold with both teams snorting
like flogged horses, with captains and coaches
effing and jeffing at backs and forwards,
talking steam, screaming exhausting orders,

[84]

that's not breath coming from my bloke, it's smoke.
Not him either goading the terraces,
baring his arse to the visitors' end
and dodging the sharpened ten-pence pieces,
playing up, picking a fight, but that's him
cadging a light from the ambulance men,
loosing off smoke rings, zeros or halos
that drift off, passively, over the goals
into nobody's face, up nobody's nose.
He is what he is, does whatever suits him,
because he has no highfalutin song
to sing, no neat message for the nation
on the theme of genius or dedication;
in his passport, under 'occupation',
no one forced the man to print the word
'custodian', and in *The Faber Book
of Handy Hints* his five-line entry reads:
'You young pretenders, keepers of the nought,
the nish, defenders of the sweet fuck-all,
think bigger than your pockets, profiles, health;
better by half to take a sideways view,
take a tip from me and deface yourselves.'

A Week and a Fortnight

Tricked into life with a needle and knife
but marked with the cross in the eye of a rifle,
laid from the first in the grave of a cradle.

Fed with the flesh not the fur of a peach
but bruised in the garden, tripped in the street,
bunged with a bottle of petrol and bleach.

Nursed at the breast on the cream of the nipple
but branded for keeps with the print of a fist,
buffed with a handkerchief, flannelled with spittle.

Baubled and bangled from ankle to wrist
but milked for a season, stung by a cousin,
dunked for a bet on the hob of an oven.

Picked for a prize for the fair of his face
but kicked to the foot from the head of the stairs,
buckled and belted and leathered and laced.

Spared from a stunt in the mouth of a lion
but dabbed on the foot with a soldering iron,
stabbed in the palm with a smouldering stub.

Left for an hour with booze and a razor
but carted by ambulance clear of the woods,
saved at the last by drugs and a laser.

Days for the dirty, life for the lost,
the acts of mercy and the stations of the cross,
the seven acts of mercy and the fourteen stations of the cross.

The Two of Us
(after Laycock)

You sat sitting in your country seat
with maidens, servants waiting hand and foot.
You eating swan, crustaceans, starters, seconds, sweet.
You dressed for dinner, worsted, made to measure. Cut:
me darning socks, me lodging at the gate,
me stewing turnips, beet, one spud,
a badger bone. Turf squealing in the grate –
no coal, no wood.

No good. You in your splendour: leather,
rhinestone, ermine, snakeskin, satin, silk,
a felt hat finished with a dodo feather.
Someone's seen you swimming lengths in gold-top milk.
Me parched, me in a donkey jacket,
brewing tea from sawdust mashed in cuckoo spit,
me waiting for the peaks to melt, the rain to racket
on the metal roof, the sky to split,

and you on-stream, piped-up, plugged-in, you worth a mint
and tighter than a turtle's snatch.
Me making light of making do with peat and flint
for heat, a glow-worm for a reading lamp. No match.
The valleys where the game is, where the maize is –
yours. I've got this plot just six foot long
by three foot wide, for greens for now, for daisies
when I'm dead and gone.

You've got the lot, the full set:
chopper, Roller, horse-drawn carriage, microlight, skidoo,
a rosewood yacht, a private jet.
I'm all for saying that you're fucking loaded, you.
And me, I clomp about on foot from field to street;
these clogs I'm shod with, held together now with segs
and fashioned for my father's father's father's feet –
they're on their last legs.

Some in the village reckon we're alike, akin:
same neck, same chin. Up close that's what they've found,
some sameness in the skin,
or else they've tapped me on the back and you've turned round.
Same seed, they say, same shoot,
like I'm some cutting taken from the tree,
like I'm some twig related to the root.
But I can't see it, me.

So when it comes to nailing down the lid
if I were you I wouldn't go with nothing.
Pick some goods and chattels, bits and bobs like Tutankhamen
    did,
and have them planted in the coffin.
Opera glasses, fob-watch, fountain pen, a case of fishing flies,
a silver name-tag necklace full-stopped with a precious stone,
a pair of one pound coins to plug the eyes,
a credit card, a mobile phone,

some sentimental piece of earthenware,
a collar stud, a cufflink and a tiepin,
thirteen things to stand the wear and tear
of seasons underground, and I'll take what I'm standing up in.
That way, on the day they dig us out

they'll know that you were something really fucking fine
and I was nowt.
Keep that in mind,

because the worm won't know your make of bone from
    mine.

Five Eleven Ninety Nine

The makings of the fire to end all fires,
the takings of the year, all kinds of cane
and kindling to begin with, tinder sticks,
the trunk and branches of a silver birch

brought down by lightning, dragged here like a plough
through heavy earth from twenty fields away.
Timber: floorboards oiled and seasoned, planking,
purlins, sleepers, pelmets, casements, railings,

sacks of sweepings, splinters, sawdust, shavings.
Items on their own: a fold-away bed,
an eight-foot length of four-by-two, a pew,
a tea chest – empty, three piano legs,

a mantelpiece and a lazy Susan,
a table-top, the butt of a shotgun,
a toilet-seat, two-thirds of a triptych,
a Moses basket with bobbins in it,

a pair of ladders, half a stable-door,
a stump, one stilt, the best part of a boat,
a sight-screen stolen from the cricket field,
a hod, a garden bench, a wagon wheel.

We guess the place, divine it, dig a hole
then plant and hoist and pot the centre pole –
tall, redwood-size, of the telegraph type,
held tight with guy-ropes, hawsers, baling wire –

and for a week it has to stand alone,
stand for itself, a mark, a line of sight,
a stripe against the sky. Steeple, needle,
spindle casting half a mile of shadow

at dusk, at dawn another half-mile more.
Held down, held firm, but not to climb or scale;
strung, stayed, but with an element of play –
in wind the top nods inches either way.

Thing to surround, build around, or simply
the solid opposite of a chimney.
Symbol, signal, trigger for those people
who deliver all things combustible

this time of year, who rummage through attics
and huts, cellars and sheds, people who check
the yards and feet and inches of their lives
for something safe to sacrifice, figures

who visit the site, arrive with a box
and set it down like a child's coffin, or
those who come after dark, before first light,
with black bags that are bursting with something

and nothing. Rolls of oilcloth are carted
by hand. A furlong of carpet appears
that must have been brought here by van. Some kid
comes a mile and a third, uphill, to tip

a hundredweight of paper from a pram,
and a man turns up to empty a bin,

does so, picks through the garbage, finds a thing
or two – a ball of string, a leather shoe –

loads up and takes his findings home with him.
Later still that man comes back with a rough
half-full half-empty sack of low-grade coal –
offensive now within this smokeless zone –

and lugs it, wears it draped around his neck
like a dead foal, one hand hold of each end,
then on his knee he lays it down. Two coals
run out like two rats across the hard ground.

Such comings, givings, goings. Morning finds
the pole upstanding through a tractor tyre –
half a ton, those, so how did that get there?
All else scattered, as if dropped from the air,

litter brought from somewhere else to right here
by act of God or twister, washed ashore and beached
by long-shore drift and gale-force winds
and a hard night of high seas. Flotsam. Dreck.

We stack the fire at the eleventh hour,
begin by propping staves and leaning splints
against the centre-piece, build up and out
from slats and rafters through to joists and beams,

take notice of its changing shape: a cairn
becoming wigwam, then becoming dome,
becoming pyramid, then bell, then cone.
It has its features: priest-holes, passageways,

a box-room, alcoves, doors. We hide and hoard,
stack bales of paper soused in paraffin
within its walls, stow blankets doused in oil,
load every seam with goods – goods to take hold –

and thread each flash point with a length of rope
soaked through with petrol, kerosene or meths
and trail the loose end to a distant place.
Unnecessary, but a nice touch, though.

That moment, then, before the burning starts –
like waiting for the tingle in the track
before the train, or on the empty road
before the motorcade, the time it takes

each elephant to wander from lightning
to thunder. That, or something in the bones
or in the weather, on the wind, a twinge
within the works of some barometer,

shouts of timber in the coral canyon
of the ear, the smell of burning pouring
through the chambers of the nose, a voltage
in the glades and groves of cells and glands. Hands

hang fire, hang loose in pairs of leather gloves,
and coolant flows and fills the trunks and roots
and limbs and leaves and needles of the lungs.
Then someone makes a move, a match gets struck . . .

The hiss first of damp wood, the fizz of steam,
a water-coloured flame, cradled and cupped

in a sheltered place, then circled and snuffed
by a twist of smoke. Something else flares up,

then chokes – a flame blown out by its own breath –
and a third and fourth are checked. More smoke
without fire, then a further space alive
with light, a chamber deep inside aglow

for good this time, fuelled with the right stuff,
feeding on something for just long enough
to tempt another thing to burn, combust,
to spread its word, to chatter its own name

through a stook of canes, to start a whisper
here and there that spreads across the broad base,
a rumour handed down, passed round and shared.
Heat dealt to every point, backed up by flames.

Sounds – the popping of corn, cars back-firing.
And sharps and flats, affricates, fricatives,
screams, an acetylene torch igniting,
a pilot light – its circular breathing.

The animal squeal of air escaping.
Snapping of soft wood – the bones of babies.
The depth-charge of a blown-out metal drum.
A pressurized can goes off like a gun,

at which a fox cuts loose from the fire, there
then gone, having waited this long to bolt
like a ball of light that breaks from the skin
of the sun; that explodes then dies. Like so,

observed through special telescopes, that is.
Lit from the front, the faces we wear
are masks, and bare hands hang down from their cuffs
like lamps. Heat to our hearts, but we each feel

the bite of frost from the nape of the neck
to the heels, a cold current through the spine
despite a hugging of duds: Russian dolls –
two shirts, three jumpers, jacket, anorak,

topped by an uncle's outsize overcoat.
A lending of heat and light to the air
but splinters of ice in our hands and hair.
Nothing to swing the weather vane, no breeze,

but down an avenue of silent trees
a dog walks a man through a rain of leaves.
Far detail: a goods-train hauling road-stone
wheel-spins at a set of signals. Diesel.

An hour later, though, the fire deep-seated,
up to speed, at full tilt. A garage roof,
bituminous, slides forward in the heat.
A window pops from its frame. A small girl

paddles in the puddle of her own boots,
melted to her feet. A man with an oar
comes forward from the crowd with a bauble
or a silver orb on its outstretched blade –

a cooking apple cased in baking foil –
which he expertly lays at the white heart

of the flames. 'For eating, later,' he says,
then stabs the fire and swipes the leading edge

of the burning oar no more than an inch
or so from the hat on the balding head
of his brother-in-law. Then shoulders it,
carries it like a banner, turns around,

and then ditches it, pitches it forward;
the sharp end finds the earth, digs in, goes out.
A grown man singes his eyebrows and screams.
And a wet dog sings in a cloud of steam.

A man who is blind walks down from his hill,
through the woods, having sensed a form of light
on his face when he raised his head, and heard
convected cinders raining on his roof.

A decent blaze, he says, but a shadow
of those in the past, of course, in the days
when smoke was mistaken for night, when fires
would singe an eyebrow from a mile away

or roast a chestnut hanging on its branch
or brown the skin through several layers of clothes.
One year his sister wore a floral blouse;
the next that she knew she was tanned with shapes

of bluets, goosefoot and morning glory.
Fires so full of the sun that each brought on
a second spring, an autumn flowering
of lilies, sesame and panic grass

and feverfew. And sickle senna too.
Another year a farmer drove a herd
of bullocks through the flames, and some came through
unscathed, but others fell, and ribs and steaks

were there to eat for those who wanted them.
But worst, the season he remembers most,
when seven children in a paper chase
holed up inside the mound of bric-a-brac

to be fired that night, and slept. And the rest
was a case of identification
by watches and lockets, fillings and teeth.
Someone gets the man a drink, and a seat.

And buildings swim in the haze of the heat.
And rockets set out for parks and gardens
and nose-dive into purple streets. And sparks
make the most of some moments of stardom.

And flakes of ash and motes of soot float up,
cool down, fall out, then go to ground. No sign,
no trace, unless they settle on the skin,
unless they come to hand or find a face

to brush or smudge or dust or break against.
And panes of glass take a shine to the fire,
and glass to all sides is amazed with light,
and every surface of a similar type

carries a torch, becomes inflamed. And eyes
if they blink are ablaze on the inside.

Gunpowder battles it out in the sky
where rockets go on unzipping the night.

Two or three at a time each firework blooms,
opens up fruits of sodium yellows
and calcium reds, shades of strontium
and copper – copper green and copper blue.

The tease of a paper fuse, then gunsmoke
shot with potash fumes, and cordite nosing
out of every empty barrel, casing,
tube. And several figures surround each squib,

and each and every huddle of people,
adults and kids, is the cast and crew
of its own short film, fifteen seconds long
at most and flickering – not black and white

but tinted in tones of alloys and chromes.
A soundtrack of sibilants, clacks and clicks,
and thuds and shrieks that are harder to place –
warfare or birdsong, peacocks or bombshells,

air raids, kittiwakes. And familiar sights,
like a Catherine wheel escaping its tail,
a Roman candle that snowballs the moon.
Clear skies, a night with its lid taken off

but peppered and strafed with fractals and flak,
gerbes and Saxons, star shells, Mines of Serpents,
Bengal Lights and other coruscations,
and the fire, glazing every act and scene

with versions of orange and tangerine,
the woods to the east thrown over with pink
and with crimson. There are cats in those woods,
they reckon, wild ones. Cats, and also mink,

but no one alive to swear they've seen them.
And a wheel of cheese – the moon on the rise,
caught like a ball in the branches of trees.
And a heat so solid now, a hard glow

we take for granted, easy come and go,
light years away from the era of flint
and stone and steel, the friction of dry sticks, the times
of trees ignited by bolts of lightning,

the untouchable gold of lava flow,
stories of sparks more precious than pearls
thrown up from the hooves of careering colts
or buffalo, struck from the beaks and claws

of eagles and hawks, and the days of flames
kept secret and safe in temples and caves.
Fire borrowed from neighbours and given back,
caught from the burning tail of a wild cat,

brought from the sun in the beak of a wren
or got from the glint in a precious gem.
Or fire snapped like twigs from red-berried trees,
bought from the otherworld, sought in the hearts

of warm-blooded things, under the stoat's tongue,
pulled from the nail of an old woman's thumb.

Burton Library
24hr Renewal Line
Tel: 0345 330 0740

Vat Reg. No GB280061977

Items that you have checked out

Title: My sister, the serial killer
ID: 38014111708985
Due: 08 September 2023 23:59

Title. Selected poems
ID: 38014111463219
Due: 08 September 2023 23:59

Total items: 2
Account balance: £0.00
Checked out: 2
Overdue: 0
Hold requests: 0
Ready for collection: 0
Messages:
OK
18 August 2023 15:43:22

Thank you for using Self Serve

General enquiries please call
0300 111 8000
Thank you for visiting Your Library
www.staffordshire.gov.uk/libraries

A distant cry from this surplus of heat,
as easily raised as falling asleep.

But then by one degree the brightness fades.
A fraction at first, it has to be said,
but then again the sun must pass its best
and move through noon the second that it strikes,

and in the space it takes to check a watch
another inch of time gets dropped, slides by,
is lost. The way it is with peaks and troughs –
that's how it goes with energy and clocks.

So we look to ourselves for something to burn,
to slow up the countdown of Centigrade,
but come up with metal: bedsteads and prams,
chains and a kettle, a bicycle frame.

A team of brothers walk further afield
to check the meadows of the north-north-east,
to comb the copse to the west of the creek,
to trawl for driftwood on the lakeside beach,

to haul the sunken jetty from the tarn,
then make a final circle of the town
and lift the stacks of litter from the streets.
They amble back with the following things:

a sack of potatoes going to seed,
a peacock feather, the skull of a sheep.
Thrown on, the feather shrinks then disappears,
the sack of spuds rolls over, waters, weeps;

with flames for eyes, the skull keeps its own shape.
Someone has to be to blame, so a man
who hasn't pulled his weight, who feeds his face
with coffee and cake is taken away.

Midnight is closing in. In steel-cap boots
and a boiler-suit, the friend of a friend
turns amber embers over with a spade,
splits wood in search of heat, looks for a pulse

within the charred remains of logs and stumps.
A girl who is said to be deaf and dumb
comes forward with a pitch-fork and a brush
and turns and sweeps the margins of the flames

for seeds and knots and crumbs, chippings and thorns
that fizz and fry an inch above the heat,
then stops, then looks, then javels both the tools
into a fire that isn't hot enough

to detonate the bristles of the brush
or separate the two halves of the fork
by rapidly unseasoning the splice.
She backs off to a darker, silent place.

We stand in profile, figures from an age
before the dawn, paintings on a cave wall,
a people waiting for a word or sign,
one of the tribe to whisper something like

when one thing dies begin again inside;
look for it in the heartbeat of the tide,

wade in the coves and bays along the coast,
between the toes. Plot the zones and borders,

map the suburbs, boroughs, claim the polders,
sift the rapids five or six times over,
trace the water courses, mark the passes
and the gorges, plant and farm the ocean,

mow the steppes and fens and string the bridges
out between the contours of the ridges,
pick and pluck the cobweb of the matrix
of the districts, fly, align the air-strips,

take a section, make a transit, chart it,
pan the Gulf Stream, dive, way beneath the hull,
then rise towards the light until the head
comes up against the ice-cap of the skull . . .

But we have given all of what we own
and what we are, and it has come to this:
this spot, this date, this time, these tens of us,
all free but shadowless and primitive,

no more than silhouettes or negatives
or hieroglyphics, stark and shivering.
A half-life, heat-loss at a rate of knots,
an hour at most before the very last.

All lost. Until it dawns on one of us
to make the most of something from the past.
He walks us to a garage, picks the lock
and pinpoints with a torch a heavy cloth,

asbestos, woven, terrible to touch,
then covering his mouth against the dust
that blinks and glitters in the beam of light
he drags the cover from a wooden cross.

No time for measuring the shortest straw
or drawing lots. There's mention of a name,
and singled out the strongest of us bends
and takes its length along his spine, its frame

a crude flying machine, as someone says,
and takes its width across his arms and neck,
its point of balance bending him double
with dead weight as he walks, or rather wades.

And children point and poke fun at his shape,
this tottering man, like a living grave.
Even the dog at his side cocks a leg.
An aeroplane mimics him overhead.

We guide him to the left towards the site
through ginnels where his wing-span clips the sides
of houses, makes a xylophone of pipes
and railings, drum-rolls on a picket fence

and likewise once again along a length
of paling, then through parkland, puddles, sludge,
the tail-end ploughing, paying out a groove
between his footprints planted in the mud,

then onto concrete paving where he halts
above a hopscotch pattern sketched in chalk.

And there he falls, but stands up straight and walks
beneath a window where his mother waves

and calls his name, warns him to tie his boots
or lose his feet. He climbs a dozen steps,
then rests, by leaning with his arm outstretched,
hand flat against a wall. For a short while

we take the strain, but he loads up again
and makes for the faint light at the far end
of the lane, where a woman seems to wait
to produce a handkerchief trimmed with lace

from inside her sleeve, and to wipe his face.
He drops a second time and then a third,
but rounds the final corner on his knees
and kicks for home when he sees the remains

of the light and heat, and raises the cross
to its full height, and hugs it like a bear.
Upright, it seems to have doubled in size.
Whatever he wears is filthy and torn,

the pins and needles of splinters and spells
are under his nails and deep in his hands
like thorns. And when he tears himself away
it stays, held up by nothing more than air.

However, mass like that, the sort, weighed flat,
to break a back or trip a heart attack,
amounts to nothing stacked; and yet a hair
can trigger it, a tap from something slight

can topple it, say timber and it tips.
In this case someone serves up half a brick
that clips the crosspiece on the left-hand arm;
it twists, turns face about, tilts and quickens,

mimics the act of launching a discus,
the east and west of its cardinal points
beginning to roll, its axis falling
out of centre, out of true. Then it lands –

a noiseless splashdown in a pool of ash
invoking a mushroom of sparks and chaff
that takes its time to winnow and settle,
to clear. Hats in the air, and a loud cheer.

And it simmers and stews in its own steam,
then ignites. Those expecting an incense
of palm and cedar, the scent of olive
and cypress, are surprised by the odour

of willow and oak and pine and alder,
resins and oils from the Colne and Calder
that babble and lisp as they mix with fire.
Warmth for an hour, but not a minute more.

And blackness follows every burst of flames
that leaves us cold again, hands pocketed,
outdone, outshone, left in the shade by stars
that boil with light when the dark inflames them,

put to shame by shapes and constellations
that were dead and countersunk and buried,

hammered home in deep space. Like the new view
of the full moon, on full beam, in full bloom,

the open silver flower of the moon,
the boulder of the moon or the moon's shield,
hallmarked with valleys and rivers and fields,
the streams and snakes and fossils of the moon,

the long plumbago nights and graphite days,
the mercury seas and mercury lakes
of the moon, the moon on a plate, the date
and the name and the make of the full moon.

Under which we figure out the next move.
Off to the west, at the boarding kennels,
low down in the fringe of the sky, level
with chimneys, the crowns of trees and pylons,

a star, four-sided, breaks the horizon –
light in the shape of a dormer window –
and out of its frame a man emerges,
naked and bald and mad, head and shoulders,

and says his piece, shouts the odds about dogs
and vomit, fools returning to folly,
and the hounds in his keeping fratch and fret
or clatter the mesh of his twelve-foot fence.

And on the one hand someone rattles off
the preconditions, lists them one by one:
for little, wedding, middle, index, thumb,
read pressure, discharge, friction, action, heat

of any kind. But on the other hand
the things we're up against: clay, fibro, lime,
the silicates and tungstates, certain salts
and sodas, borax, alum; more than five,

not counting water and things of that kind.
Scissors cut paper and paper wraps rock,
rock blunts the scissors but water, water
swamps and dulls and rusts and dampens the lot.

Nothing else for it. The tightest of men
makes a move for his wallet, goes through it
for fivers, tenners and twenty-pound notes
and lets them drift to the little that's left

of the incandescence, like petals, picked
for the purpose of proving love, or not.
Another takes a last look through a deck
of snapshots, passport-size, in black and white,

then deals that pack of thirteen photographs
to the fire, the way some poker player
sits and tosses cards into a cocked hat.
And each image burns with a true colour.

Another burns a book of stamps, a cheque,
a calling-card, goes through his pockets, finds
and flings a ticket stub, a serviette,
a driving licence, birth certificate.

Another pulls a hip flask from his side,
empties it out on a mound of briquette;

the liquid vaporizes into scent:
angelica, wormwood, star-anise, mint.

He turns to us and tells us what it is
or what it was, and then pockets the flask.
Another strips his friend of his flat cap,
prizes it from him like a bottle top,

then slings it, frisbee-style, into the ash.
Another man decapitates himself
or so it looks from here, beheads himself
it seems, unzips the detachable hood

from his coat for the sake of the lost cause,
looks for a naked flame, and on it goes.
And on it goes: a pair of gloves, a scarf,
a balaclava lifted from a face.

The act of keeping warm by burning clothes –
like eating your own hand to stay alive
or tapping your arm for a quart of blood
to survive. Tell that to the starving, though,

and the dry, those of us feeling the cold
tonight. We follow suit, burn every stitch
for one last wave of heat, pixel of light.
Unbuttoned but thankfully out of sight

except in the eye of the moon, silent
except for the padding of feet, bare feet,
we turn to go, then go together, home
in numbers, then in pairs and then alone

to houses ransacked and reduced to stone,
uncurtained windows, doors without doors,
to rooms that are skeletal, stripped, unmade,
to beds without cover, lamps without shade.

At dawn, through living daylight, half asleep,
we drift back to the place, which brings to mind
a crater punched home by a meteorite
or else a launch-pad or a testing-site.

Kicking through the feather-bed of ashes
someone flushes out a half-baked apple.
Softened, burnt and blistered on the skin, but
hardly touched within. Inedible thing,

the flesh gone muddy, foul, the core and pips
that no one cares to eat still fresh, still ripe,
and him who found it heads off down the slope
towards the park and plants or buries it.

We wait, listless, aimless now it's over,
ready for what follows, what comes after,
stood beneath an iron sky together,
awkwardly at first, until whenever.

from MOON COUNTRY

Song of the West Men

To the far of the far
off the isles of the isles,
near the rocks of the rocks
which the guillemots stripe
with the shite of their shite,

a trawler went down
in the weave of the waves,
and a fisherman swam
for the life of his life
through the swell of the sea

which was one degree C.
And the bones of his bones
were cooler than stone,
and the tide of his blood
was slower than slow.

He met with the land
where the cliffs of the cliffs
were steeper than sheer,
where the sheep had to graze
by the teeth of their teeth.

So he put out again
for the beach,
and made it to lava
that took back his skin
to the feet of his feet,

and arrived at a door
with a tenth of a tale
that was taller than tall,
as cold and as bled as a man
from a fridge. But he lived.

The good of the good
will come this way, they say:
tattered and torn,
unlikely and out of the storm,
if it comes at all.

from CLOUDCUCKOOLAND

A Glory

Right here you made an angel of yourself,
free-falling backwards into last night's snow,
indenting a straight, neat, crucified shape,
then flapping your arms, one stroke, a great bird,
to leave the impression of wings. It worked.
Then you found your feet, sprang clear of the print
and the angel remained, fixed, countersunk,
open wide, hosting the whole of the sky.

Losing sleep because of it, I backtrack
to the place, out of earshot of the streets,
above the fetch and reach of the town.
The scene of the crime. Five-eighths of the moon.
On ground where snow has given up the ghost
it lies on its own, spread-eagled, embossed,
commending itself, star of its own cause.
Priceless thing – the faceless hood of the head,
grass making out through the scored spine, the wings
on the turn, becoming feathered, clipped.

Cattle would trample roughshod over it,
hikers might come with pebbles for the eyes,
a choice of fruit for the nose and the lips;
somebody's boy might try it on for size,
might lie down in its shroud, might suit, might fit. Angel,
from under the shade and shelter of trees
I keep watch, wait for the dawn to take you,
raise you, imperceptibly, by degrees.

The Tyre

Just how it came to rest where it rested,
miles out, miles from the last farmhouse even,
was a fair question. Dropped by hurricane
or aeroplane perhaps for some reason,
put down as a cairn or marker, then lost.
Tractor-size, six or seven feet across,
it was sloughed, unconscious, warm to the touch,
its gashed, rhinoceros, sea-lion skin
nursing a gallon of rain in its gut.
Lashed to the planet with grasses and roots,
it had to be cut. Stood up it was drunk
or slugged, wanted nothing more than to slump,
to spiral back to its circle of sleep,
dream another year in its nest of peat.
We bullied it over the moor, drove it,
pushed from the back or turned it from the side,
unspooling a thread in the shape and form
of its tread, in its length and in its line,
rolled its weight through broken walls, felt the shock
when it met with stones, guided its sleepwalk
down to meadows, fields, onto level ground.
There and then we were one connected thing,
five of us, all hands steering a tall ship
or one hand fingering a coin or ring.

Once on the road it picked up pace, free-wheeled,
then moved up through the gears, and wouldn't give
to shoulder-charges, kicks; resisted force
until to tangle with it would have been
to test bone against engine or machine,

to be dragged in, broken, thrown out again
minus a limb. So we let the thing go,
leaning into the bends and corners,
balanced and centred, riding the camber,
carried away with its own momentum.
We pictured an incident up ahead:
life carved open, gardens in half, parted,
a man on a motorbike taken down,
a phone-box upended, children erased,
police and an ambulance in attendance,
scuff-marks and the smell of burning rubber,
the tyre itself embedded in a house
or lying in the gutter, playing dead.
But down in the village the tyre was gone,
and not just gone but unseen and unheard of,
not curled like a cat in the graveyard, not
cornered in the playground like a reptile,
or found and kept like a giant fossil.
Not there or anywhere. No trace. Thin air.

Being more in tune with the feel of things
than science and facts, we knew that the tyre
had travelled too fast for its size and mass,
and broken through some barrier of speed,
outrun the act of being driven, steered,
and at that moment gone beyond itself
towards some other sphere, and disappeared.

The Winner

When the feeling went in the lower half of my right arm
they fitted a power-tool into the elbow joint
with adjustable heads. When I lost the left
they gave me a ball on a length of skipping-rope
and I played the part of a swingball post
on a summer lawn for a circle of friends.
After the pins and needles in my right leg
they grafted a shooting-stick onto the stump.
When septicaemia took the other peg
I thanked the mysterious ways of the Lord
for the gift of sight and my vocal cords.
With the brush in my teeth, I painted Christmas cards.
When I went blind, they threaded light-bulbs
into the sockets, and slotted a mouth-organ
into the groove of the throat when cancer struck.
For ears, they kitted me out with a baby's sock
for one, and a turned-out pocket, sellotaped on.

Last autumn I managed the Lyke Wake Walk,
forty-odd miles in twenty-four hours – oh Ma,
treasure this badge that belongs to your son
with his nerves of steel and his iron will.
This Easter I'm taking the Life-saving Test – oh Pa,
twenty-five lengths of the baths towing a dead weight,
picture your son in his goggles and vest, with a heart
like a water-pump under a battleship chest.

For the Record

Ever since the very brutal extraction
of all four of my wisdom teeth,
I've found myself talking
with another man's mouth, so to speak,
and my tongue has become a mollusc
such as an oyster or clam,
broken and entered, licking
its wounds in its shell.

I was tricked into sleep by a man with a smile,
who slipped me the dose
like a great-uncle slipping his favourite nephew
a ten-pound note, like
so, back-handed, then tipped me a wink.
I was out with the stars,
and woke up later, crying,
and wanting to hold the hand of the nurse.

Prior to that, my only experience
under the knife was when I was five,
when my tonsils were hanging
like two bats at the back of a cave
and had to be snipped. But that
was a piece of piss compared with this,
which involved, amongst other things,
three grown men, a monkey-wrench

and the dislocation of my jaw. I wonder,
is this a case of excessive force,
like the powers-that-be evicting
a family of four, dragging them
kicking and screaming, clinging to furniture,
out through their own front door?
Like drawing all four corners of the earth
through the Arc de Triomphe.

You might think that with all the advances
in medical science
teeth like these could be taken out
through the ears or the anus,
or be shattered like kidney stones
by lasers from a safe distance.
But it seems that the art
hasn't staggered too far since the days

when a dentist might set up his stall
at a country fair
or travelling circus.
I'm also reminded of John Henry Small
of Devizes, who put his fist in his mouth
but couldn't spit it out,
and the hand was removed, forthwith,
along with his canines and incisors.

Returning to myself, the consultant says
I should wait another week at least
before saying something in haste
which at leisure I might come to repent.

But my mouth still feels
like a car with its wheels stolen, propped up
on bricks, and I'm unhappy about the way
they stitched the tip of my tongue

to my cheek.

Homecoming

Think, two things on their own and both at once.
The first, that exercise in trust, where those in front
stand with their arms spread wide and free-fall
backwards, blind, and those behind take all the weight.

The second, one canary-yellow cotton jacket
on a cloakroom floor, uncoupled from its hook,
becoming scuffed and blackened underfoot. Back home
the very model of a model of a mother, yours, puts
two and two together, makes a proper fist of it
and points the finger. Temper, temper. Questions
in the house. You seeing red. Blue murder. Bed.

Then midnight when you slip the latch and sneak
no further than the call-box at the corner of the street;
I'm waiting by the phone, although it doesn't ring
because it's sixteen years or so before we'll meet.
Retrace that walk towards the garden gate; in silhouette
a father figure waits there, wants to set things straight.

These ribs are pleats or seams. These arms are sleeves.
These fingertips are buttons, or these hands can fold
into a clasp, or else these fingers make a zip
or buckle, you say which. Step backwards into it
and try the same canary-yellow cotton jacket, there,
like this, for size again. It still fits.

from The Whole of the Sky

The Mariner's Compass

Living alone, I'm sailing the world
single-handed in a rented house.
Last week I rounded the Cape of Good Hope,
came through in one piece;

this morning, flying fish
lying dead in the porch with the post.
I peg out duvet covers and sheets
to save fuel when the wind blows,

tune the engine so it purrs all night
like a fridge, run upstairs
with the old-fashioned thought
of plotting a course by the stars.

Friends wave from the cliffs,
talk nervously from the coast-guard station.
Under the rules, close contact
with another soul means disqualification.

Hydra

At the jungle research station in Manaus, they keep
a brown electric eel in a dishwater-coloured goit,
that looked to me, when it was pointed out, more like
a dead palm-leaf, or, side-on, a length of gutter pipe.

But as I said to the man who was showing us round,
dingy or not, you have to take your hat off to a beast
that keeps itself to itself for the most part, but when touched
transforms a single thought into several thousand volts.

Hercules

After not taking the cat to the vet's for a jab,
not putting the garden hose back in the garden shed,
not tracking something down, not bringing bacon home,
not blacking the kitchen stove with black lead,

after not finding the dead bird the cat smuggled in,
not not talking bullshit on the phone all day to friends,
not paying the blacksmith cash instead of a cheque,
not bringing the washing into the house when it rained,

after not having the spine to dig the vegetable patch,
not picking the fruit before the fruit went bad,
after not walking the dog once all day for crying out loud
I collapsed, exhausted, on my side of the unmade bed.

The Centaur

In a dream, climbing the path towards Hill Farm
I count the steps – railway sleepers set into the bank,
holding the earth back. In the stable I hear
the flick of a tail, hooves on a concrete floor.

I crash a topstone through the frozen water trough
and dredge the ice. Then walk, unbolt the door,
and raise the bucket of smoke and broken glass
into the warm, dark space, up to your human face.

Leo

I first worked as a supermarket warehouseman,
hand-carting greasy boxes of butter into a dark cellar.
It made me a better person than if I'd been born
with a gold mine under the pillow. All this went on

under the rooftop statue of a stone lion, blackened with soot.
During a power-cut, the council switched the cat
for its fibre-glass brother, yellow and hollow,
which at sunrise charmed the town with its depth of colour.

Andromeda

I've had dealings with some real hard cases on the stairwells
and landings and wings of Her Majesty's prisons, spied
through peepholes putting names to faces, exchanged syllables
with bombers and bank-robbers, person to person.

But once I got stuck in a cell with him
who bound and gagged the rich man's daughter, left her
tied to a ledge in a pitch-black well or a drain.
And nobody came. And nobody came.

The Stern

My heart went out to the Falklands widow, screwed
by the Falklands hero with medals and wounds, the bloke
whose cover was blown on the day he referred
to the back of the boat as 'the back of the boat'.

Portsmouth Harbour in '82, an afterthought.
The fleet making its way, sharp end first, trailing
a wake in its wake, setting out for the south.
The shape and the taste of the heart in the mouth.

The Eagle

At the country house, he lay face-down
on the gravel path as they drove the bird in a van
to the top of the hill, into the sun. They opened the doors
and it circled and dropped, and he felt the shade of its wings,

its claws locking into his ribs – keratinized, diamond-tipped.
Then it ate from the handful of meat in the small of his back.
This feather, leaf of the sky, finger to fly with,
he kept to himself as a thing to get by with.

The Lynx

All night, a presence outside in the gardens and grounds,
drawn to the house by the stench of a secret.
Keen-eyed, looking in through the walls, a big cat, sensing
irregular breathing, a surge in the nervous system.

At dawn, a walk on the frozen, fibre-glass lawn, an inkling
of acetone, pear-drops, methadone linctus.
Beyond the ferns on a cobweb slung between two thorns,
eight beads of urine hardened into eight discoloured pearls.

The Keel

Three nautical miles into the North Atlantic
I rocked backwards. The sea flapped and heaven shook out
its thick grey blanket. Mr Maxwell, in yellow oilskins,
saw the ship's knife open a codfish like a drawstring.

I climbed below deck through the boat's eardrum.
A school of whales went past like a thought.
In the medicine-chest of the darkest room – the boom
of the body of ocean under the trawler's breastbone.

The Phoenix

Tvillage cuckoo wer caught one spring
to trap tgood weather, an kept in a tower baht roof.
Tnext mornin tbird'd sprung; tMarsdeners reckoned
ttower wernt builded igh enuff. A ladder wer fetched

to bring tbird dahn, but nubdy'd clahm.
Trust, tha sees. Tladder maht walk. Chap maht be stuck
in clahdcuckooland till Kingdomcumsdy, Godknowswensdy.
Meanwahl, tbird wer nested in Crahther's chimney.

The Ram

Half-dead, hit by a car, the whole of its form
a jiggle of nerves, like a fish on a lawn.
To help finish it off, he asked me to stand
on its throat, as a friend might ask a friend

to hold, with a finger, the twist of a knot.
Then he lifted its head, wheeled it about
by the ammonite, spirograph shells of its horns
till its eyes, on stalks, looked back at its bones.

Capricornus

On my first visit to the Yorkshire Avalanche Dodgers,
they brought in a shaggy old goat by its handlebars,
which was Ronald Dyson's, or it was Ronald Hodge's.
I was thinking of knives and blood, but it opened its arse

and the president counted its turds as a kind of raffle.
There were thirty-one, as it happened, excluding
globular clusters, nebulous objects and other dark matter.
The goat breathed in through its horns as Harry Ronson

sent his hand in search of his missing five-pound-note
as far as his elbow into the sleeve of the animal's throat.
On a later visit, we ate chicken served from a shopping-basket
and thick-cut chips passed round in a bucket.

Canis Major

Walking north over the hills, we were joined by a dog
that wouldn't turn back for twenty or so miles
despite the beating it took from one of the lads.
Feeling bad, we reckoned we'd all stump up for a cab

to take it south when we got to a road, but half-killed
it limped ahead to a house where it happened to live,
which happened as well to be our digs for the night.
So it died quietly under the table as we ate.

Lepus

Mist, asleep like poison gas
in the valleys underneath. But up here
clear skies, where the mind comes up
from the deep, lighter than air.

With a girl's fist for a head,
second-hand fur, kangaroo legs: a hare,
triggered out of the earth
in a triple-jump sprint, keeps up with the car.

The Fox

Standing its ground on the hill, as if it could hide
in its own stars, low down in the west of the sky.
I could hit it from here with a stone, put the torch
in the far back of its eyes. It's that close.

The next night, the dustbin sacked, the bin-bag
quartered for dog meat, biscuit and bone.
The night after that, six magpies lifting
from fox fur, smeared up ahead on the road.

Horologium

Slap bang on the equator, my Citizen solar-powered watch
thought all its Christmases and birthdays had come at once,
and rather than having to drag the present out of the past
it was having a hard time of it holding itself back.

With the sun looping the loop, there might have been no use
for a timepiece at all, but I set its luminous hands for home
because at night, which came down fast, new constellations
to the south made strange sideways movements, like troops.

The Water Snake

We sat on the green bank at the side of the road,
passing the time with the girl who wanted to top herself
but somehow managed to stop herself
from driving her mother's car into the stream below.

The cops were called on a mobile phone, and came,
but not before the village fire-brigade, eight men
with cartoon bodies and animal heads, hell-bent
on doing something useless with the hose, the hose

which had, as they say, a mind of its own. Alive,
and way too strong for the one with the donkey's face to hold,
it stood up straight, spun round, and spat at the girl,
the girl who wanted to die but was too wet now and too cold.

The Air-Pump

Bored with squirting helium into the children's balloons,
we started passing round the metal bottle, toking
on the nozzle, talking out of our arses, gassed
with the most noble of the noble gasses.

We were spacemen in their space-suits, somehow,
or inner tubes. Then steadily, the way shipwrecks are raised
from deep ocean fissures, we drifted up through the everyday
towards our four intended and described positions.

Leo Minor

When pictures came through
of the world's first authentically green cat,
I was out of touch, watching
in black and white on a rented set.

I thought of my mother at home
the day Kennedy was shot,
in rubber gloves, crying real tears
into the washing-up.

Canis Minor

The porcelain dog that we brought from the cupboard
with its tell-tale coat for predicting the weather:
quite simply blue for snow, gold for summer.
Winter sunlight on the day my sister wonders

if her little Einstein, two years old, holds good
with this world and its signs and seasons, or another.
The heirloom glazed with a sense of the future –
where is it now, in whose hands, and what colour?

The Flying Fish

Blue-backed, silver-bellied, half-imagined things;
six of them, blown off course by the solar wind.
They were coated with salt or snuff – interstellar dust –
and we picked the granules out of their tails and wings.

We carried them out to the beach in a budgie cage,
lowered them down and opened the door. They went deep,
then turned about, breaking the surface, launching themselves
whole-heartedly out of the sea at their own stars.

The Chisel

You and him, a two-man chain-gang, making sparks by shaping
millstone grit to raise a wall. When split, each rock
lets fly its smithereen of heat, except this stepping-stone
of ganister, a cubit long each side, that will not give.

You hold the chisel in a double-handed fist. He lifts
the hammer up above the ridges and the peaks, brings home
the height of Puddle Hill, Scout Head, Pole Moor, West Nab,
onto the nub of steel, into the metal nib.

Sagitta

From nowhere and nothing, a man was slashed in the face
with a Stanley knife one evening. The blade opened him up
between the eyes and across both lips. Police
say the slashing had no motive and no meaning. Fate,

travelling headlong forwards, ground to a point.
But to stare into space is to stare into history.
Whatever comes at the Earth at the speed of light
will be here upon us, then beyond us, instantly.

Crux

Some kid at school died when he split open his head
on the metal stilt under the music room. Next day
some kid marked the place with an X or a cross
next to the two hairs stuck with dried blood to the spot.

In a life, most of us turn no more than 45 degrees. Not much
compared to those who turn full-circle in the slightest breeze
or those who totally uncoil, but enough in the end
to tell a bag of diamonds from a sack of coal.

from KILLING TIME

§

Meanwhile, somewhere in the state of Colorado, armed to the teeth
     with thousands of flowers,
two boys entered the front door of their own high school
     and for almost four hours
gave floral tributes to fellow students and members of staff,
     beginning with red roses
strewn amongst unsuspecting pupils during their lunch hour,
     followed by posies
of peace lilies and wild orchids. Most thought the whole show
     was one elaborate hoax
using silk replicas of the real thing, plastic imitations,
     exquisite practical jokes,
but the flowers were no more fake than you or I,
     and were handed out
as compliments returned, favours repaid, in good faith,
     straight from the heart.
No would not be taken for an answer. Therefore a daffodil
     was tucked behind the ear
of a boy in a baseball hat, and marigolds and peonies
     threaded through the hair
of those caught on the stairs or spotted along corridors,
     until every pupil
who looked up from behind a desk could expect to be met
     with at least a petal
or a dusting of pollen, if not an entire daisy-chain,
     or the colour-burst
of a dozen foxgloves, flowering for all their worth,
     or a buttonhole to the breast.
Upstairs in the school library, individuals were singled out
     for special attention:

[153]

some were showered with blossom, others wore their blooms
    like brooches or medallions;
even those who turned their backs or refused point-blank
    to accept such honours
were decorated with buds, unseasonable fruits and rosettes
    the same as the others.
By which time a crowd had gathered outside the school,
    drawn through suburbia
by the rumour of flowers in full bloom, drawn through the air
    like butterflies to buddleia,
like honey bees to honeysuckle, like hummingbirds
    dipping their tongues in,
some to soak up such over-exuberance of thought, others
    to savour the goings-on.
Finally, overcome by their own munificence or hay fever,
    the flower-boys pinned
the last blooms on themselves, somewhat selfishly perhaps,
    but had also planned
further surprises for those who swept through the aftermath
    of broom and buttercup:
garlands and bouquets were planted in lockers and cupboards,
    timed to erupt
like the first day of spring into the arms of those
    who, during the first bout,
either by fate or chance had somehow been overlooked
    and missed out.
Experts are now trying to say how two apparently quiet kids
    from an apple-pie town
could get their hands on a veritable rain-forest of plants
    and bring down
a whole botanical digest of one species or another onto the
        heads
    of classmates and teachers,

and where such fascination began, and why it should lead
        to an outpouring of this nature.
And even though many believe that flowers should be kept
        in expert hands
only, or left to specialists in the field such as florists,
        the law of the land
dictates that God, guts and gardening made the country
        what it is today
and for as long as the flower industry can see to it
        things are staying that way.
What they reckon is this: deny a person the right to carry
        flowers of his own
and he's liable to wind up on the business end of a flower
        somebody else has grown.
As for the two boys, it's back to the same old debate:
        is it something in the mind
that grows from birth, like a seed, or is it society
        makes a person that kind?

§

Why don't we start again from the top, from the head:
    dream up a new cult, think of a new force.
Time collects. Time passes, but not with the tread
    of footprints in sand or tyres along a road
or a train on the East Coast line, passing a junction box.
    Time collects, accumulates, gathers together,
remains to be seen. Time thickens, coagulates, clots;
    what lies at your feet is its sediment,
piled from the core to the surface, forming the ground.
    Time builds up in layers: up there
is the clean, unknowable future waiting to rain down
    or fall out, waiting to drop. The present,
the here and now, extends from our minds to our toes,
    from the crowned heads to the down-at-heel,
from verrucas to brain tumours, haloes and frontal lobes,
    from our snoods to our air-cushioned soles.
But underground is the past. Below stairs –
    that's where dust and bone
and pollen and skin and rust and soot and fibre and hair
    and splinter and soil are packed hard,
becoming stone, becoming rock, becoming earth.
    And not just things we can measure
and weigh, items of proof, material worth,
    but sounds and visions,
echoes and views – they lie here in the stone,
    jammed into silence
and blackness by time, by its billion billion tons,
    time laying down its load.
The great geology of time. The gravity of loss.
    And memory lies here too.

Memory – the glue of time, bonding it close,
        the gel that splices
one split second to the next, the gum that sets the past
        in solid form, binding it shut,
holding it monumentally hard and fast.
        So history can be opened again,
but not by force. Plastic explosive will fail
        to worm time from its shell;
hard labour, hammer blow, pulverization, blade and file,
        reduction of solid form to its powdered state
will not release time, neither will high-voltage connections,
        magnets, particular wavelengths of light,
nor pinning-down under powerful lenses, looking at sections slice
        by slice, or baking hard in a kiln.
Time will not be extracted like ore
        from its mother-rock, like mercury
from cinnabar, or drilled from the planet's core.
        Only water will work.
Water that makes its way down, reaches back to the first.
        Water which mimics the action of time,
which makes for the lowest point; that is its task, its thirst.
        The world over, water is working
its trick: conjuring up whatever is unseen and unsung.
        Atoms of history boil up
into the air, vaporize into the lungs.
        Hold it there. You are keeping
yourself in breath with the dates and figures and facts
        and lives and losses and loves
of a history smothered by dust. You are breathing the past.
        Make it real again, because
this is the cycle to which we are all born.
        We journeyed ashore

to set the past free, to release the secret of time from stone,
    uncurl the stubborn fist of what is gone,
to flood the rocks that hold the limited supply of time,
    to irrigate memory
and float the great, revolving permanence of humankind.
    Look down at your feet, which are fish.
Imagine everything locked in time's keep,
    everything buried, enshrined, encrypted, encoded, entombed
in sleep. Now, bring back the dead. Breathe deep.

from THE UNIVERSAL HOME DOCTOR

Incredible

After the first phase, after the great fall
between floorboards into the room below,
the soft landing, then standing one-inch tall
within the high temple of table legs,
or one-inch long inside a matchbox bed ...

And after the well-documented wars:
the tom-cat in its desert camouflage,
the spider in its chariot of limbs,
the sparrow in its single-seater plane ...

After that, a new dominion of scale.
The earthrise of a final, human smile.
The pure inconsequence of nakedness,
the obsolescence then of flesh and bone.
Every atom ballooned. Those molecules
that rose as billiard balls went by as moons.
Neutrinos dawned and bloomed, each needle's eye
became the next cathedral door, flung wide.

So yardsticks, like pit-props, buckled and failed.

Lifetimes went past. With the critical mass
of hardly more than the thought of a thought
I kept on, headlong, to vanishing point.
I looked for an end, for some dimension
to hold hard and resist. But I still exist.

Index of Titles